ABOUT

NETWORK MARKETING

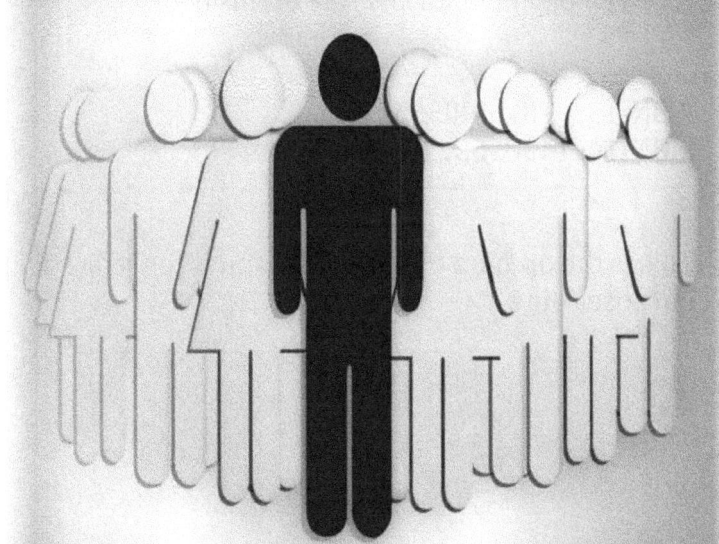

LISETTE TOPPING
KEEPING IT STRAIGHT SERIES

Copyright © 2013 L Topping

All rights reserved, including the right to reproduce this book or portions thereof in any form whatsoever without written permission.

Note: Sale of this book without a front cover may be unauthorized. If this book was purchased without a cover, it may have been reported to the publisher as "unsold or destroyed," neither the author nor the publisher may have received payment for the sale of this book.

ISBN-13: 978-1490555218
ISBN-10: 1490555218

This is the opinion of the author and is for reference purposes only.

Table of Contents

Forward 3
A Few Facts 8
What is Network Marketing 12
Why It Works 17
Check the Company 21
Here's a Heads Up 25
What to Expect 29
Beware of Pyramid Schemes 38
Don't Follow the Dollars 42
Some Drawbacks 46
Facing Reality 56
Why You Need to Keep Pressing 65
How to Keep Moving 72
Final Thoughts 78
Recommended Reading 80

Forward

This is information that no one who is trying to recruit you into a Network Marketing or Multi-Level Marketing business wants you to read. I wrote this in an effort to enlighten people have had a bad first experience to what could be an otherwise profitable path if they were first educated on the topic.

Why you'll need this? A friend, family member, advertisement or perfect stranger will approach you with an opportunity claiming it will change your life. There is truth in what they're saying because they have seen it happen to others, or it could have happened to them. What is often missing is the process that you will have to go through to get there. Now, what you will have to ask yourself is "Am I ready for that change?"

Keeping it Straight

This is the information you need in order to lower your risk of failure. It will fill in the blanks your potential recruiter did not have the time, knowledge or heart to tell you. There is nothing fancy or complicated here; it just shines a spotlight on the good, the bad and unknown of network marketing. You will get some facts, stories, downfalls and secrets to help you make your choice wisely. The goal is to **Keep it Straight**.

When approached, the good stuff is all they'll talk about. How much you can make, how easy it is, all the wonderful things they have to offer and why it's the greatest opportunity out there. The feeling of being doomed to a life of mediocrity comes over you (many are stuck in this place and don't even know it), and you want to be free from it.

There is **The Almighty Disclaimer**; "These results are not typical, join at your own risk!" Wealth, health, freedom and happiness will not be achieved by the masses.

Use this to assist you to compare opportunities based on logic instead of emotion. Know what to expect, what to ask, and understanding the pitfalls before you join in.

There are books and reports that will tell you about the industry, how to choose a good company, and what scams to look out for. It's all basic, you may get the idea that the danger is minimal and effortless, so why not try? Let this be your first warning: The money and time invested can become very costly, if you value these you better take notes. Second, most small businesses fail within their first few years. The numbers are worst here because of how easy it is to get involved and it's that much easier to walk away.

There are hundreds of network marketing companies out there to choose from. They market everything from products, services and ideas. The compensation plan will vary, and some terms will be different. The basic concept is the same "through direct sales, people bring people to an opportunity."

Before you read on any further, please be advised that the decision to join a Network Marketing/MLM business is far from a personal decision— even if the invitation to join comes by way of a close friend or family member. It is a professional and business decision that requires an initial investment. You invest money to make money. Whether your initial investment is large or small, you want to make a return on that investment. Network Marketing is about making money, and if you're not informed about how the industry works, you'll learn the hard way that the money and more importantly the time you invest can become very costly.

With that said, get ready to take some notes.

- ✓ You will be prepared to take part in and take advantage of a business model that has been around for decades, and will continue to be around.

- ✓ You will be able to make an educated decision on which company to work with.

- ✓ Take a view on your life that you may not have looked at before

A FEW FACTS ABOUT NETWORK MARKETING COMPANIES

Network Marketing is not a new concept!

The origins of network marketing companies go way back to the early 1900's. In fact, a few of the earliest network marketing companies are still around today, and are pretty much household names.

The California Perfume Company had 10,000 sales representatives and 117 different products as early as 1906. Today we know it as Avon Products. Ring a bell?

The California Vitamin Corporation began selling products way back in 1934. Today we know it as the thriving vitamin supplement company Nutrilite Products Company, Inc.

Then there's what might be the most commonly-known network marketing company of them all, which launched back in

1945. That company was the Tupperware Party Plan. It's a billion-dollar company that has its products in cabinets and refrigerators in households spanning 40 countries.

Network Marketing Companies are not just privately owned business ventures!

Although some network marketing companies are privately owned, many are publicly traded on the stock market. A few of the publicly traded network marketing companies that you're probably familiar with are: Avon Products, Herbalife, Tupperware, and PRIMERICA, INC

(to name a few).

Keeping it Straight

Network marketing Companies offer multiple ways to get paid!

Network marketing companies present a lot of opportunities for you to make money. You can earn money by directly selling products, earning a percentage off the direct sales of products sold by people you introduce to the company, providing training to people new to the company, selling your network of customers to someone else, earning residuals on certain kinds of products or services, and/or earning bonuses offered by a company. Of course that was a general description. We'll get more descriptive later on in this book.

Network Marketing is a $180 billion global industry!

Amway Corp. made 9.5 billion in sales in 2015 alone. You could've easily been one of Amway Corp.'s sales representatives and gotten a slice of that huge pie. The revenue is there, and this book is about helping you prepare to decide if it's worth your while to try to get a share of it.

WHAT IS NETWORK MARKETING

Network marketing /multi-level marketing (MLM) is a combination of direct sales and franchising. Individuals come in as independent contractors and earn money from the sales they make personal or sales made from their team of people they have recruited and developed for the company. *Boring*

To state plainly: You have a company that has products/services to offer and they use word of mouth advertisement from groups of people and/or individuals to promote this product/service instead of spending advertisement dollars. You make money from your sales, the sales of people you help join the company, a percentage off of any ongoing sales made from the customers who have come through your group and often times various bonuses. You can build your own distribution network within the company itself.

Network marketing is a people business, point blank. Every business is a people business. A business needs people to create, supply and buy. Companies that choose this method feel that using people to advertise their products and rewarding them with sales commissions and recruiting bonuses, is a win-win solution. It has been shown to be an efficient and effective method of distributing products and services. The system has proven to work because there are some very successful Network Marketing companies that have been around over 40 years, and paid out billions of dollars in compensation to individuals that partnered with them.

So, is it legal? *Yes.*

Does it work? *Yes.*

Does that mean it's a good deal? *No!*

Keeping it Straight

Not a good deal without some general information to help you choose wisely.

This ideal situation for this to work centers around you telling some friends, and they tell some friends, and this repeats indefinitely. This creates a network of people who are connected through different levels of association coming together for the benefit of selling or using a product/ service. They're **uplines**, **downlines,** and in some cases **sidelines**. The levels are created as individuals join the opportunity and branch out to get others involved. You are a team of individuals who work together to help each other achieve their goals. *Ideally again,* this is how it should be. Connecting together to change lives, hopefully for the better.

Here is the plus side: You don't have to figure out how this works and what to do by yourself. You'll find people who will invest their time to assist you. Some will only be doing it because there is a monetary gain, but there are people who genuinely care about your success and have nothing to gain financially. If or when you find these types of people you have something priceless. In the end, again it's all about a network of people being connected through a common desire to market a product or opportunity that can change individual lives and fulfill their dreams.

How it starts:

Anxious Adrienne was approached by Best Buddy Barry. Barry was so full of excitement about some information that he heard and wanted to share. Even though Adrienne had no idea of what he was saying she decided to listen in on a recorded phone call he gave her.

Now Barry is just starting out and is doing what he was told. He wanted the incredible lifestyle that was painted for him. Cousin Calvin introduced him to this information and so far has had some success with it.

What is now developing is a small team. Calvin being in the position of what is call an **upline** to Barry. Barry is a **downline** of Calvin. Barry's will be an **upline** to Adrienne if she decides to join. Adrienne's would be a **downline** to Barry.

Why It Works

The concepts behind network marketing are ***residual*** income and ***leverage***. This is what makes it a successful and lucrative business model. Instituting these two things in business can make you rich no matter what the industry is. Real estate, insurance, medical, television, publishing and franchises are some of the industries that use this business model. If you can keep getting paid over and over from a single effort or sale, and multiply those efforts through other people or media, you can become wealthy.

Most network marketing companies offer either products or services. Here's why: With consumable products, products that have to be purchased over and over again because they have been used up, a customer gets accustomed to them and their benefits and would want to continue using it. They are going to purchase more from you because these products are generally offered through independent distributors only. With a service, you have to pay some kind of ongoing fee to maintain the service. This way you get a little percentage each time someone pays the fee or buys the product.

This works if you have a real product that is not overpriced, or a service that you just can't look-up and get the same quality at a competitive price.

So, it's not the business of network marketing that's bad, but there are some bad network marketing companies (really bad). Start understanding these things and you can figure out how to weed out the bad ones.

Another reason why it works is because they have removed internal rivalry that can go on within a company/industry. Here's how: In the real estate industry, many brokers end up training their competitor. In retail, you have senior employees who are not inclined to train new hires because this can hurt their commissions. And in other industries, nobody wants to train their possible replacement.

This is not the case in Network Marketing. You benefit from helping others you bring in because you earn an ***override***. That way if you train them to be good at doing the business you can continue to earn money as they earn money. In some companies you may also have training bonuses. These are just some of the incentives that are given to those who are there to help others.

You can also get paid by recruiting people to join the company. **Please be very careful with this one here** (more on this later).

You should be able to make a nice income off the sales of product or service in the event that you don't want the responsibility of having a team of people, or talk to people about the opportunity it is still worth getting involved.

In traditional business it would be like having a bunch of franchises or distribution centers. The more stores you have in a location, the more customers you are able to serve. You just don't have the brick and mortar overhead to do it this way.

Check the Company

Knowing who you are going into business with cannot be emphasized enough. The more independent information out there, the better it is for your research for your decision making process. You have to deal with a company that you can do some real research on. You need to know how long they have been in business, the industry they are participating in, how much they are worth, where are they doing business, and how much they are earning annually. But most importantly how much commission is being paid out. What good are big sales numbers if they are not paying anything out to the distributors?

If it's publicly traded that's good, because that means they have to report what they are doing and earning, this is public information. If they have a Dun & Bradstreet report to look at, check it out. Use the BBB (Better Business Bureau) and/or whatever governmental agency that governs their industry. You want to deal with companies that have an established track record. They have to report their goings and comings to an outside entity that keeps track of them. If you can't find this kind of information on them, look out, because they can disappear and no one will ever know they even existed.

If it is not publicly traded, that doesn't make it a bad company. Your research may be a little more difficult. "Google" is the easiest place to start when you don't know where to start. What you want to look for is what major media empires are saying about them, not individuals. Look for what publications or other media outlets have reported because they have a research department to get the facts.

They have an obligation and a lot more to lose if the facts are not correct.

Investigate who is running the company and what's their history. Are they leaders in the industry? What's their mission and how long have they been with the company? The heart of the company will be the heart of the person running it. You can have an idea of how the company is and where it's headed by who is leading them.

How long the company has been around is really, really important. You don't want to deal with a company that is a start-up. The idea behind them may be a good one, but time is needed to get operations and structures established. Take a look at the dot com period. At that time a whole lot of companies had plans for greatness, how many are still around now?

Don't fall for that **"get in on the ground floor", the floor has not been tested to see how much weight it can hold.**

Your research will be the hardest part. Who really wants to take the time and look up countless information on a company? If there are entities that have already done the research, move on, don't get stuck here. There is more work ahead, but it's easier when you don't have to convince people on the company's credibility. Articles or websites will make things easier.

The reason this is an important step if you are just starting out is because your future is at stake. If it's a new company and big money is made quickly, you may start living those big dreams (car, house, vacation, tuition, etc) and the company disappears, so does everything that was attached to it.

Here's a Heads Up

If you haven't paid attention to anything else you've read thus far, I suggest that you do so now because this is where it gets real interesting. I'm about to tell you how to spot a set-up. If someone comes using any of these things I'm about to tell you, listen with caution. Hear what they have to offer. The product or service just might be worth your while. Unfortunately, the "opportunity" might not be.

Possible Pitches

"Come join us, and have 'X' amount of people you know join, and they do the same with 'Y' many people and you will have financial freedom."

Keeping it Straight

What they don't tell you is that getting that many people and KEEPING that many people to continuously stay active in the business is the problem. They will be able to give you phenomenal numbers on how much you can make, and even have a few people who are actually making that kind of money. But the reality is, there are plenty of people who will not be able to recoup the money they initially invested, not because the program didn't work, but it's because they didn't. Well, that's not actually a fair assessment. You will have to constantly keep putting people in the "pipeline" as they call it because you will have to replace people that drop out along the way.

"No one else does it or has it like we have it. You will not find a company like ours."

You have to have something unique to separate you from the rest. If it's a nutritional product, there has to be some claim that can be made why it's better than what is on the market. If it's a service, it has to do something that no one else is offering and/or doing at that price. Whatever it is, it has to be different so don't make their uniqueness be the only thing that grabs you and pulls you in. That special ingredient in that unique product will eventually find itself the hot subject in another product, patent with another way with a different company. They will find a way to do it better, faster and/or cheaper. So in other words, that idea, product, service, berry, herb, juice or pill can become successful enough to get the attention of a major company and produce it for the general consumer.

The claim of being different is not limited to a question of products and services. The compensation (meaning commissions) will be different because of pricing, production and/or payout structure. Some will give you a larger payout in the beginning, others may level it out, or it may depend on volume sold.

At the end of the day it goes back to doing your research. The pitch is to get you interested. Research is where you learn if it's worth taking that interest to the next step.

What to Expect

From Yourself

To succeed at doing this you will have to try selling, telling (sharing is the word used), and compelling people.

Sell them on whether it's the opportunity to own a business and change their life or the product/service that will improve their life. Persuasion will be an art you will have to develop for this arena (remember I stated there is a process). Persuading is a skill we acquired early in life. Our parents were our first customers. We were always trying different methods to get them to look at our point of view, same concept just a different area. You'll paint the picture, sing a tune and even dance a little to get their attention for your pitch. "Dangle that carrot."

Keeping it Straight

In a lot of cases, they'll be buying "you". Your excitement, passion and friendship are your tools of the trade, use them. These will be the reasons they will at least hear you out.

With no newspaper ads or television commercials to get the word out, this is the assignment you have chosen.

Tell them what they are getting into and what it is going to cost them. This is a real business they can have for themselves, make the kind of income they desired, and be able to dictate what they are worth. This will be hard for many people to understand since this was not taught or explained in a traditional setting. Unfortunately the amount of money in their pockets and bank account are all they can see as the value they are worth. You're trying to erase that by explaining how you hope what you have found will be beneficial to them and they can see beyond what they have become to know as their life.

Compel is the hardest thing to do of the three. This is where having them take action on the opportunity comes into play. That there is a business model that has people helping people reach goals that they couldn't do on their own or working for someone else. The low cost investment that some of the companies ask to join can cause many to wonder how it is possible to get the type of returns they are being told is achievable.

Understand that being told you can make a million dollars off of a couple of hundred dollars sounds like something that can land you in jail, to say the least. They are definitely going to want proof that this is possible. It helps when you can also show real life examples of others who have made it within the company.

One thing it may cost you is the respect of family and friends who can't understand why you would get involved with this, let alone invest money in something so unheard of. How could you waste your time on such a thing?

Expect yourself to be challenged, ridicule and pushed to a new level of self-awareness. You will see how tough you are when it comes to battling for your freedom. The difference here is the greatest opponent you will be facing is yourself. You can determine the outcome of this by winning the battle in your heart and your head will figure out the rest. You will have to stay committed, focus and determined to prove your point.

From The Company

The company should provide you with all the support you need through training, technology, and administrative functions. You shouldn't have to worry about if orders are being processed on time. Most of all, you should never have to worry if you are getting paid properly. If you have any problems, whether it's with your business or a customer, live support should be available during reasonable business hours. Beware of companies that don't have a physical headquarter or facility. If all you have is an email address and a phone number where you are leaving messages consider that a clue, this may not be a stable operation. They can pick up and go at anytime without leaving a trace.

The company should be doing everything in its power to keep its name in a positive light. The worst thing that can happen is looking at the news, and seeing the company you've staked your future on involved in a scandal. At the same time don't believe every bad article you read. There is always some bad publicity on some level. That's how it is with most major companies in general, be prepared for some bad press as long as it's minor. If lives are in jeopardy and people are going to jail remove yourself immediately. Again this is if you choose to go forward.

There also has to be evolution if they want to stay in business. As the market change so should they. They have to keep providing new and improved products. The opportunity also has to keep getting better, because that will get people excited to join them and stay. Investing in their future and yours should be priority # 1.

You should be properly trained on the business, industry and products. This should be ongoing and preferably hands on. BUT…you should not be paying to be trained. I'm jumping ahead, but a sneaky way this is done is by having someone come out with you to "talk" to your people and making sales. They do this a few times and keep the commission because they did the work and were training you on how to do the business. You are told this is how training is done and you will get to do the same with your new people.Companies have training bonuses that they offer, which is fine as long as it's not at the expense of the new person not getting paid or having the people that would support their business, supporting someone else.

Another note on training, there may be outside training that is approved by the company that may not have anything to do with the company directly. If it's endorsed by the company it may be optional, but worth looking into. This is a legitimate expense which is okay, as long as it is a reasonable amount of money and the company fully endorses it.

The last thing you can expect from the company is how they stand in the industry. Are they leaders, innovators, or pioneers? What good is being a part of a huge industry and no one in the industry has heard of them or respects them. Of course, not everyone will embrace a newcomer, but again this is where your due diligence comes in handy.

The story continues:

Anxious Adrienne really was interested in what she heard, but wanted to be sure if what she was listening to was entirely correct. She decided it was best if she did some research before she immediately got started.

She went to the **business chamber of commerce** website to see what negative reports they had received and did find a couple. She checked out the **Dun & Bradstreet** report, and found the company had been in existence for over 10 years. She was also able to find articles on the internet from magazines that did some informative reports. Once she compared the type of complains to the company's history she decided that this was a good company to partner with.

But before she put up her investment money to do the business, she wanted to see if *she liked what was being offered so she joined as a customer only. The results impressed her so she decided to go for it. She was able to get family and friends to try what she was offering because they saw how well it was working for her. She stayed with people she knew because she had relationships with them and that made it easy to approach them. Not everyone felt they needed what she had, but they agreed that if they knew of others who might, she would be the one they would refer them to.*

Beware of Pyramid Schemes

The sad thing is that Network Marketing and MLM has also been called Pyramid Schemes. Unfortunately, many people have been burned by Pyramid Scams, and because of this they're not even willing to look at any information that may remind them of what they had gotten involved in. Now that you're reading this book, you've an advantage when it comes to recognizing the difference between a real network marketing business and a phony Pyramid Scam. Or, they think they know what a Pyramid Scam is and really have no idea what they are saying. Don't let this stop you from looking since you have read this book you have something in your favor (hey why not pass it on).

Here's a quick way to know that you might have come across a scam. If they say join us and you will get paid after you have recruited in a couple of people and there is no product/service option sales to get your investment back. **BEWARE!** You should have a way to get paid on the sales from your own efforts not just people from having people joining the opportunity for it to be legit.

There may be some companies with a factious overpriced product or superficial product in the background as a front, or you pay a high monthly fee for a template website they are providing. Therefore, you can't make any money off of the sales from it because the commissions are so low. They will call this ***residual income*** because you are getting paid through the fees paid on the sites month after month, but not from any products or services being provided. Understand, if you are not getting paid over and over again from having loyal customers ordering and using the product or service, this is not true residual income. Most important as I stated already, if you can't make money on sales of the products or services alone than it's likely a scam, since you will have more distributors than buyers.

Legitimate companies have products that their distributors love to talk about. They'll have testimony after testimony on how it has impacted lives. Some companies will even require you to have tried or commit to using the product/service at sign up, so you can truly understand what it is you are getting involved in and what it is you are offering. These companies have more customers than distributors.

Ask the company in question for a product presentation. Pyramid schemes will not have one, because the product is not important, or it doesn't exist. They will have an opportunity presentation talking about the money. The IRS is also using "product/service presentations" in their audits to determine if you are claiming a legitimate business.

Please also be aware of the **gifting programs** where they will say how the government allows you to give people money as a gift and try to use that to sound perfectly legal. Never send your money off to something and not have something tangible (other than a so call manual) being returned. No product or service means no real business.

If you can't make any money unless other people join, that is a serious problem, this cannot be stressed enough because they are out there, and using the internet and classified ads to trap unsuspected people who are looking for an opportunity to better their financial situation. When they get burned here, it's hard to convince them that they will not get burned again.

Don't Follow the Dollars or Follow the Products

No matter what you chose to do or use in life, it has to be a benefit one way or another. Meaning, if you are going to promote something, let it be something that you can give a personal testimony about. If you can't honestly say this has done x,y, or z for you or others you know and/or have met, then walk away, leave it alone because you don't want to give up your integrity for no amount of dollars. My advice is simple: if it is something that you feel you would be interested in doing, try it first. This way you'll be a firsthand witness, or have someone you feel needs it use it for you to see if there is really a benefit.

You can continue knowing what others may say can't affect your belief because you know what it has personally done in your life and/or in the life of others. You should be willing to refer the product, even if you were not making any money off of it. Not only that, if you can get paid off the product or service over and over again, you don't have to worry about the recruiting side of the business because money is being generated from the ongoing sales.

Honestly, it will make you more money faster if you have help telling and sharing it. Yet, there are companies that have people making six-figures selling by themselves with no team. They are doing it by telling one person or group at a time.

Let's not forget the money does count and for that reason if it's not paying like it should, use the product and don't get involved in the business side. Don't sell a $40 product and settle for getting paid $.50 because you love the product so much.

If it's the dollars that interest you, how much are you willing to spend to get it? Some companies will require you to spend certain amount, or sell so much volume to get paid. This has caused people to have an abundance of products they can't get rid of.

Some people may not see this as a bad trade off, spending a couple of hundred dollars to get paid thousands. What happens if you can't come up with the hundreds, or don't see the need in the products? How long before it doesn't sit right with you to continue doing it? Most run out of storage space before this happens. If it is a concern for you it will be a concern for others, so know how to address it. You will read more about this in **Drawbacks Section**.

Following the dollars means understanding the compensation payments which varies from company to company, as well as industries.

When comparing compensation plans, it can be complicated. Some will speak in terms of true dollar amounts, others will use sales volumes, and there are scales of what payments will be based upon your level within that company.

Only you can determine if you are being paid enough for the service and work you are providing.

Some Drawbacks

Price to Start

No matter what type of business you go into there will be some kind of cash investment. A large investment to get started is something to look out for. The cost of starting can vary. You may pay as little as $10 to join, or as much as a few thousands. If you cannot get a return on your money after a few product sales, or fast start bonuses, then think again. The thing you want to show people is that with some effort, they can see a profit. Even if it's just a dollar more than they put in, turn a skeptic into a believer.

Breaking off A Piece

Check if the company requires you to pass a portion of your team to your *upline*. This can hurt you, especially if that was a major part of your income and sales volume. You will need to know how to plan for this. The term is sometimes called **breakaway**.

Pass You By

You may stop getting override income on a person you've brought in because they have reached the same level as you, or has passed your level. You should be on the lookout for your rising star. This should motivate you to keep ahead of them because you know there is money to be made. Companies do this also to motivate people to go to the next level. Again not all companies do this, but you should include this as part of your investigation or research.

You Have To Buy First To Get Paid

You are the middle person between the company and customer. You may have to purchase the product and deliver it to the customer. Proceed with caution. Why? You can get stuck with some products in the end. People will conveniently forget that they placed an order. They don't have the money at the time it comes in. It may not be what they had expected and to return it may be more trouble than it's worth. Sometimes your schedules will not be in sync to make the delivery and collect payment.

Have a place for extra inventory, or a re-sale plan. Ebay or a flea market may be an option.

You will see less of this thanks to the use of on-line order placements and payments. Companies are now delivering the products directly.

Watch For Quotas

Companies that require you to make so much in sales over a recurring period in order to get paid are out there. This has cause individuals to stockpile products, so they can meet their quota for a check or get paid at a higher commission level. They have accumulated so many products that they can't sale them quick enough. There goes money they can never get back. If a person decide to leave and their portion of the sales have to be made up by you in order to remain at a certain level for commission payment. The smarter solution would be to recruit more people into the business.

The Money May Not Be Yours to Keep

You are paid when a product or service is sold, but if for any reason a person chose to cancel or request a refund. What goes in your pocket will come out of your pocket. That can be painful if no one warns you of this possibility. So be aware that the company giveth and the company can taketh away. In most instances the company generally takes it back from future sales.

You Just May Have to Learn This on Your Own

It's possible that the person who introduced you to this business, may be in another state or even another country, so the support you need may not be face-to-face. Make sure that there is enough support via phone, internet, or company events that you can get the training and support you need.

If you are the type that needs some hand holding, there maybe someone locally you can connect with.

Not In All States

There may be some states where you cannot promote your business because of government regulations. Know which ones they are. That way you can target your market accordingly.

You may have to get licensed or pay some kind of fee to do business in other states, so again check this out. The process may be too hard or the fees too high. Check with the company to see what the guidelines are in each of the areas they operate.

No Double Dipping

Companies are very serious about you leaving their company and trying to recruit those same people to your new venture. Make sure you understand that if you decide to leave, you cannot have your team leave with you to your new opportunity. Be prepared to start over.

Also, you may not be able to work two network marketing companies at the same time. The reason is because you could be taking customers or recruits from the other company.

You should commit your efforts to one company if you want to be successful, because you don't want someone you are interested in doing business with see you as someone who can't commit or unfocused.

Not an Opportunity for Everyone

Everyone may not be able to join due to past situations, or certain affiliations. Check out what are the requirements to join. You don't want to get someone excited about this wonderful opportunity, and the company informing them they cannot work with them.

How it Ends:

Best Buddy Bob told everyone he met about the wonderful opportunity that he found. The more people he told, the more "No thanks" he heard. What he quickly figured out was that a few people said "Yes" and that turned into a lot of money for him.

For every person that did say "Yes" that lead him to more people he didn't know. This helped his organization grow very big quickly. Now, it just wasn't him telling stories, but plenty of individuals in different place were helping him. He was earning a little bit of commissions off of a whole lot of people, and everyone was happy because they were making money.

On the other hand, you have Cousin Calvin who had some success, but not on the level of Best Buddy Bob.

What Calvin failed to realized that just like in traditional business you can't rely on one customer to sustain your business. It takes more than one highly motivated person for your financial dreams to come true.

Anxious Adrienne was completely happy with the additional few dollars she was earning a month through repeated orders from customers and referrals. This allowed her to plan for extra things that her regular income would not allow her to afford.

Facing Reality

This section is to help you understand that there are some things that cannot be avoided, once you've decided to join a company. I understand that you are reading this to decide if this concept is for you, but you have to know some of the pitfalls before you do decide to sign up.

No Work, No Pay

People will bad mouth network marketing, because they have never tried network marketing as a business. Let me explain. We all do network marketing when we recommend a movie, barber, product or service, we just don't get paid for it. So we can't say network marketing doesn't work because we do it day in and day out. What happens is when you do it as a business you have to go out and tell people about it to get paid. I don't care how great, wonderful, awesome, or terrific what it is you are trying to sell or do is, YOU DON'T TALK ABOUT IT TO OTHERS YOU WILL NOT GET PAID.

It's Not Everyone Desire to Have More

As strange as this may sound you will find individuals who have all the cash, time and freedom they need and are not looking for more. The waterfall of money is flowing in their backyard and they don't need to look at anything else. Yes, they are out there. They are alright financially and they have enough time on their hands to enjoy that money.

Don't Worry About Friends and Family

You may become part of the N.F.L (No Friends/Family Left). Unfortunately, you may have to forsake all to follow what is in your heart. This may possibly be the hardest thing to deal with when starting out. Even if you do succeed, they still may not want to join you. Understand this in the beginning, because you may think it's you, but it's not. Some will be expressing their views out of love because they don't want to see you fail. Others may not want to see you doing better than them. After all, why should you be the first crab out of the barrel? This may be the one time you don't have to worry about doing business with friends and family.

You May Have Brought Them to the Sun, Doesn't Mean They'll See the Light

Moses brought a whole nation to the promise land and many didn't see it. You create the picture, bring them in, they follow you, and they believe you until they see a little obstacle, get a rejection, or lose faith in the opportunity or themselves. You can't make people do what seems so obvious to win. You can bring them in, but you can't make them work. That is why you have to repeat the process of finding more.

Always remember:

Some will

Some won't

So what

Next

Most companies will tell you 2 out of 10 will get it. You will have to go through a lot of no's to find you one yes.

This Maybe Your First Try, but It May Not Be Your Last

Many successful people have tried and failed at many things before they found success. The same will be true for most when it comes to network marketing. The model has been proven, but sometimes things are not a right match. You will hear people who have made a great deal of money with a company tell you that this was not their first try at it. That is a good thing to know to keep you looking, searching and trying. Just because the shoe didn't fit you, doesn't mean there is something wrong with the shoe, it just wasn't your size. Try other shoes until you find one that fits.

Plan To Put In Some Hours

Full-time income on part-time work will happen after you have done some full-time effort for part-time income. Read the stories on those who have made it in "brick and mortar" business and they will tell you how they worked long hours with no pay so they could reinvest in their business. It was a sacrifice, but it paid off.

To really get paid you will really have to work in the beginning, the reward maybe small because you are starting at the bottom of the compensation scale, but you will reap the benefits if you stick around and WORK AT IT!

They May Not Listen the First Time

Let me give you another warning here. A lot of people you approach have been approached by others in the past and are very resistant to even hearing what you have to offer. It's better hearing it twice from you, then hearing first from another and start working with them. There is nothing more hurtful than seeing someone you know join the company with someone else.

You will find yourself talking to the same people over and over again just to have them look at what it is you are offering. Not many people buy after seeing the commercial the first time.

Keeping it Straight

There are exceptions in which life has been kind to some of them because they have the financial security they need for themselves and their family. Circumstances may change. If the time comes for them to look for options yours might just be the thing they need.

*As a side note about the latter group of financially secure people, they also understand opportunities and having additional income coming in, so seek them out and ask for their opinion on what it is that you are trying to accomplish."

Your Goals May Not Be Theirs

You may feel the need to express the opportunity, since it seems everyone can use extra cash. The incredible huge amount of income that can be earned a month may turn people off because they can't see themselves doing that.

A little extra money to ease up the financial burdens they are going through may be all that they want. The secret is to let them tell you the desires of their hearts and take it from there. People are committed to a goal they've set and not feel the pressures of living up to levels that others have set.

Some Things Are Not For You to Change

People have to be ready to do something about their situation in order to *do something about their situation.* For a vast majority this is the case, but there some factors to consider:

Pride will not allow them to be open to the possibilities that someone can help them with their circumstances.

Doubt will have them believing that nothing can be done, this is just how their life is suppose to be. It's hard for them to think believe can get better.

Complacent to the way things are. They don't seek to change because they are satisfied where they are and what they have.

Fear is the greatest of them all. It will keep them locked in the "life of lack". They will not step outside of what is comfortable for them, to discover what may be best for them.

Why You Need to Keep Pressing

Endless Possibilities

Unlike a job, the possibilities of making the kind of money you dream of or need are here for the making. You will be a witness, and associate with people who are doing it. Know that you can work at your job and your future, but your income is always dictated by someone else.

Look at your boss or others, are they enjoying life or just existing? Do they have time to enjoy the money they are making? Are they living the life you hope to have? How many years will you have to work to achieve it? Think of what this opportunity can do for you if you really work at it, and decide if it's worth it. Anything in life worth having is worth working for it.

Time Freedom + Financial Freedom = Total Freedom

Many people would love to have more time to do what they want, but that could come at a sacrifice of making money. To make the kind of money they want, they may have to offset that with time.

Having time to do what you want, with the money to do it with, is priceless. We all understand that time is the one thing we spend and never get back, why spend it someplace where you're not getting the greatest return?

Lack of time also equals stress. Without time to do what you enjoy doing is just being a slave to the clock. This is why the financially successful will look at this with a different set of eyes. For every hour we work it can be equated to a dollar amount. So when you command a high price per hour and find something that can substitute that with less effort you should investigate it, at least.

Financial freedom will be the biggest selling point for most people. People would do more if they had more. The stress of not having enough funds has torn many families apart. People are tired of limiting their dreams according to their pockets. They want the freedom to choose where to vacation, where to live, what school to send their children and charities they could help.

When you have both— total freedom has been achieved. The ability to do what you want, when you want and having the money to do so, is the greatest freedom in the world. You will be able to upgrade some things in your life. People who love to do charity work can follow their hearts and those who want to give can do so without looking at their pockets. Your world will become a whole lot bigger and so will your heart.

Being Your Own Boss

You can throw away the alarm clock and plan your work around your day, not plan your day around your work. If you need a raise you know what YOU have to do to get it, not rely on someone else telling you if you can/cannot receive it. Take the day, week, or month off if you like, you can be in control if the income is right.

This is a double-edged sword. For some the discipline of doing what needs to be done, when it needs to be done, can be too much for some people to handle. Let's face it, most of the people who work will do no more than is required. In network marketing you have to be willing to do the work because no one is watching you. Here your income depends on your efforts and what you put into determines the outcome.

Additional Security

The doctors, lawyers and professional individuals will look at this with a different set of eyes. If they stopped working today, their income would stop. Having something in the background generating another source of income, "Just in case" is an added benefit. They can see how this could also free up their time if they could replace their income doing this.

Having Options

Having the options to do more than what you are doing because you have more to do it with is priceless. You may not have the total freedom, but you can have more choices. You can sleep a little better because you have something extra coming in.

Try It You Might Like It

Because you can do this while working your job, you are not sacrificing your income. The investment is usually low so it should not be a financial hardship. This may be one of the best ways to find out if being an entrepreneur is right for you.

Cheapest Business School You Can Attend

Real business skills are what you will be learning, no matter what level you achieve. You will get to learn about marketing, training, recruiting and managing. Time management and goal setting skills will also be acquired. How to be a leader will be a part of it too. It will be up to you to learn and master these lessons that are presented to you. Learn them well, because these are not just business skills but life skills.

Your Uncle Sam Will Lend a Hand

When you join a network marketing company as someone who can offer the product or service on their behalf, you are an independent contractor. Once you generate some income you are in business for yourself.

I'm no CPA, so please consult one to verify what I'm telling you for your situation. There are so many tax advantages to having your own business, I can't begin to list them all. There is a lot of information out there on the subject, but always consult with a tax professional. There are ways to offset your paycheck, with some of the expenses you use to run your business. Things like your car, home, and travel can be considered in reducing your tax liability. This is definitely worth looking into.

You can ask how to set this up so you can get the best tax advantages.

How to Keep Moving

The purpose of this section is for those who may have tried other opportunities or feel they may not be getting the right information from the people they are involved with. This will hopefully help you stick with it. And for those who are doing this for the first time, it's just some things that may assist you.

List, Leads, Listen

If you find yourself part of the N.F.L (No Friends/Family Left), you will have to use the next 3 things to stay in business. You will have to make a ***list*** of people you know (you do know more people than your family and friends, I hope). This can be everyone from your doctor to your children teachers. The fact is there are always people around you. Always add to your list people you meet on a day to day base. You may not talk to them about what you are doing right then, but you are creating a relationship that may help in the future.

Leads can be referrals from people you know, or there are companies that you can buy them from. Caution about the second one, most network marketing companies will have a list of companies they will advise you to use. Consult with the company on that. You can get your own leads through some sort of advertising, again consult with the company for their guidelines on what you can say in your ads.

Listen for what people around you complain about or question. You will be surprise at how you may have the solution to their problem. They could be seeking to make more money, you may have the solution. They might need a service or product you offer.

Doing the Numbers

This business like every business is all about the numbers. How many times do we have to do something to get the desired results. The numbers may vary a little from person to person, or some techniques may produce better results than others. The company should have done these numbers for you, so use them to plan your time and know where to put in your effort.

If you see a company is asking you to sell some high priced item, which cannot be consumed rather quickly, than I would think again. This is not the kind of residual income you want. You would be more like a salesperson. Now this is important for you to get:

Example: You joined company A. You've just sold a high-priced item earning yourself $500, the person will not need another one for another 3 years. You were able to sale 1 a month so by the end of the year you made $6000 ($500 x 12). You've decided to do no more selling. The company will still pay you for your customer because you did refer them and you still are doing what is needed to keep getting paid, and in 3 years you get another $6000. Not bad for 1 year worth of work.

*1 year of effort after 3 years =$6,000
    Year 1 = $6,000
    Year 2 = 0
    Year 3 = 0
    Year 4 = $6000 (This is 3 years after the first year)

Now with company B you notice that you get paid about $10 a month per customer of commission for products sold or service they signed-up for, your goal was to make $500 a month. You were able to get 50 customers who agree to purchase every month in your first month ($10 x 50). Now just like the one from company A at the end of the year you've made $6000.

*1 month of effort after 3 years = $18,000
Year 1 = $6,000
Year 2 = $6,000
Year 3 = $6,000

Don't get caught up in the big payout upfront. Some will tell you it takes the same amount of work to get the high-priced item sold than a low priced item, but how often are people replacing those items? If it's not a necessity, it's not happening, and not for long lengths of time.

More Math

Because this is a business that uses leverage, you no longer have to figure out how much work you have to do to reach a certain income level. You can use the efforts and desires of the people you bring in to help you out there. One of the best ways to do this is by helping them reach the income level they want because that will automatically push yours up. The more people you can help the better. You rise when they rise!

Final Thoughts

You have to understand the potential you have at hand. You have the chance to not only change your life, but the lives of those around you—both directly and indirectly. Choose the right company, and you can create a legacy for your family for generations to come.

The main thing you have to understand is the reason why you decided on what company to join. The company has to be able to do what you believe it to do in your heart, not just the words that are part of the presentation.

At the end of the day is the lotion, potion, drink, product or service going to make a difference in a person life? Is the opportunity just as good for the person who joins today as it was years prior and will it still be as relevant years to come?

The industry may be growing, but how many companies are participating in the industry. If it's a trillion dollar industry and there are a billion of other companies in it, then your opportunity has become very small.

With all the companies out there no one person will completely be able to write on them all. With the uses of new technology the industry will continue to change and new companies and marketing methods there is more to come.

I hope that this report was useful in your search for information. Please email me your comments so I can be of better service with my information. Remember I don't know what every network marketing company has to offer or if it will work for you. This is to just help you narrow your choices and figure out what may be the best fit for you.

Recommended Reading

There are plenty of "How to" books if you decide to join this industry. These books are recommended because they talk about the industry.

The Business of the 21st Century by Robert Kiyosaki

Wave 3 Series by Richard Poe

The Ultimate Guide to Network Marketing by Joe Rubino

www.ingramcontent.com/pod-product-compliance
Lightning Source LLC
Chambersburg PA
CBHW071609170526
45166CB00003B/1029